Home is a Sweater

poems by

Stefanie Wielkopolan

Finishing Line Press
Georgetown, Kentucky

Home is a Sweater

Copyright © 2023 by Stefanie Wielkopolan
ISBN 979-8-88838-269-1 First Edition
All rights reserved under International and Pan-American Copyright Conventions. No part of this book may be reproduced in any manner whatsoever without written permission from the publisher, except in the case of brief quotations embodied in critical articles and reviews.

ACKNOWLEDGMENTS

I would like to thank Rune Literary Magazine, Heartland Review, Low Ghost Press, Nerve Cowboy, and Pittsburgh Post-Gazette for publication of selected poems in previous form.

Publisher: Leah Huete de Maines
Editor: Christen Kincaid
Cover Art: Clay Walker
Author Photo: Hsiung Leu
Cover Design: Elizabeth Maines McCleavy

Order online: www.finishinglinepress.com
also available on amazon.com

Author inquiries and mail orders:
Finishing Line Press
PO Box 1626
Georgetown, Kentucky 40324
USA

Table of Contents

Home is a Sweater 1

Snowstorm in Black Mountain, NC 2

Lemon Cake in the Fridge 3

Indoor Trees 4

Wendell Berry and Coffee 5

My Friend Finn 6

Lawn Bowling and Birds 7

Modern Art with Grandpa 8

Summer 1983 9

Untitled 10

Ancestry 12

Rendering of my Stomach 13

Suspension of Memory 15

Dim Sum in New York City 16

Cross Section of a Heart 17

Stock of Livelihood 19

The Night Before Thanksgiving in a Trader Joe's Parking Lot 20

American Thanksgiving 21

The Burning of Trees 22

We are the Pine Trees 24

Ask Me 25

Driving to East Lansing for my Brother's Intervention 26

Diorama 27

Suttons Bay, MI 28

Are You a Member of the Co-Op? 30

Berlin is a City of Borders 32

*Dedicated to my parents and grandparents,
from Dearborn to Edon, you are forever in my words.*

Home is a Sweater

Michigan is a tight sweater
snug around my chest and waist.

The neckline,
a compression of home
and the Great Lakes.

In the summer, spun wool
suffocates and
icicles puncture lungs,
in the winter.

The Detroit River
    a rum running strait
slips up and down my left arm
while one gold thread,
    sewn through my shoulder blade
    and right bicep,
whips strings
tightly around my back.
The broken phonograph
from my grandparents' attic
wraps my spinal cord
and squeezes
until the music

is finally heard.

Snowstorm in Black Mountain, NC

We shovel ourselves
out of the apartment,
pack the dog,
and drive downtown.

Our small town,
under a foot of January snow,
is shut down,
save for the Chinese restaurant
where our take-out is ready,
and the tavern
that plays bluegrass on Friday nights.

People crowd around small tables at the bar,
necks wrapped in scarves and feet in heavy boots.
Friends lean in close to each other
as they shoot back pints of beer and mugs of wine.

The *open* sign,
a reminder that we all need
a place to belong.

The bookstore and pottery shop,
    closed for the weekend,
are outlined in gold strings of light.

The windows, frosted over,
a pattern of crystal ferns and
sugared grass.

A pattern, you say, *of home.*

Lemon Cake in the Fridge
for Hsiung

I walk home from the bar
and hold close
the lemon cake
you made me.

I listen
as the snow
falls on
the foil.

The steps of my run-down
apartment
push up against the orange
winter sky.

I do not explain
the importance of moments,
you simply
know and bake.

I keep the cake
in the fridge
next to a bowl of beans
and a bag of apples.

Each time I open
the door
I think of you.

As if the cake
is a reminder
that I am no longer
alone.

As if the cake
is the center
    and I
am finally home.

Indoor Trees
    for Dad

The trees on Highway 9,
    a powdery brown and red,
remind me of the miniature trees
placed around your train table
in the basement.

As a kid, I studied the small homes
lit up by one tiny bulb,
a fireplace, and fake snow.

People gathered around the tracks,
    in the small made-up town,
sat on benches and walked
to the market.

It was another world down there,
    a kind world,
created by you. Quiet and calm.

Wendell Berry and Coffee
for Scott

The old guy walks up to me,
stares at the books on my table,
The Love of Impermanent Things and *Muskrat Friday Dinner,*
then walks away.

I glance over to his table,
two collections of Wendell Berry poems,
apricot Danish, strong coffee,
and a newspaper.

He seems to be of the grumpy sort,
rough around the edges, but sweet
to the core. Then again, maybe not.

I'm reading a meditation on aging,
then a poem by Silsbe about the Bloomfield Bridge Tavern.
It's about longing, at least I think so,
and I begin to miss Pittsburgh,
more than normal.

I feel the vinyl barstools at Bloomfield Bridge.
I hear the muffled sound of the jukebox.
I taste the pierogis and the Red Platter of kielbasa.
I see the table where we ate one night
after a poetry reading down the street,
five years ago.

The old guy gets up to grab more sugar,
glances back when he sits down.
I want to ask him if he's a writer, his favorite Berry poem,
what he likes to read. But, I'm shy,
and instead pack up to leave.

I'm late for the mechanic.

My Friend Finn
for Sage

My friend Finn dreams we are owls.

We fly around Black Mountain at night,
hang out in the trees by the railroad track
and make a nest from scraps
collected at Dairy King.

We eat breakfast with the common Finch,
compliment her worm collection,
the organic greens, her hospitality.

In the afternoon, we perch on branches above the schoolyard
and sway in silence.

This is our friendship, Finn whispers,
as he points his wing to the mountains on Route 9,
and the horses, he adds, *are our protectors.*

Lawn Bowling and Birds
    for Jess

We are closer to fifty than thirty,
an observation made as we drive around Los Angeles.

At stop signs, in between talks of breast feeding,
tired skin, baggy eyes,
we confess retirement goals.

I say: *I could really get into bird watching when I'm older.*
And you say, as any best friend would, *I can absolutely see you doing that.*

At the next intersection,
underneath palm trees,
surrounded by expensive cars, leathery women,
and overly fit parents,
we pass an urban park,
full of tan grandparents who throw a heavy ball,
down a manicured green lane.

You say: *I'm going to try lawn bowling when I retire.*

Modern Art with Grandpa
for Grandpa

My legally blind,
Depression era grandpa,
never liked modern art.

He sneered at the black canvas with one
white line
that sat at the far end
of the Modern Art room.

He despised the wall of televisions,
that played the national anthem at the top of the stairs,
and the floor to ceiling canvas,
painted entirely red.

Still, he took me
to the Detroit Institute of Arts
Sundays after church
and held my hand
as we wandered
from room to room.

Room to room,
trumpets and airy jazz
lived in our footsteps.

The smell of weak church coffee
still on my grandfather's breath.

The hall of medieval knights.
The mark of the Industrial Revolution
painted by Rivera. Humanity.

One humid Sunday,
we became the particles of paint in the air,
the sound of wet shoes on wooden floors.

The large red canvas,
the wall of televisions,
became our heart.

Backyard on Venice Street, Summer of 1983
for Mom

She is the aluminum chair
   turquoise terrycloth jumper
and two daughters splashing
in the plastic pool
next to her feet.

Untitled

Let's talk about words.

The ones we say to each other
and
ourselves.

The self-talk of: You can't be taken seriously as a person
 or an artist.
Look at your apartment,
the dust on the walls,
the onion skin on the kitchen floor,
the pile of clothes on your grandmother's chair.

Let's talk about a well-lived in,
temporary apartment that has books,
papers, textbooks, everywhere you turn. Your husband,
in his last semester of Chinese medical school,
the smell of herbs,
the unfinished puzzle on the small kitchen table,
the bills that are tacked to the wall,
the pre-natal vitamins,
the fertility medicine,
the cabinet of supplements,
the dried Chinese herbs,
the vaginal steam box: because you were/are
willing to try anything to feel better
and get pregnant.

Grasp the bedroom dresser with a drawing of your cats,
letters, poems, and pictures from your students.
Picture the sweet hamster on the living room rug that loves
watermelon seeds, spinach, and pink lady apples.

Sit next to the window and listen.
Listen to the woodpecker,
the birds that still chirp,
even in February.

Look at your bookcase,
the rows of poetry books sent to you from friends.
Books about teaching and writing.
Books that help you feel better.

Books that say, "You're ok."

You are ok.

Ancestry
> *for my grandparents*

If you unrolled my skin
          the texture of raw croissant dough
beneath the bubbles of fat and pockets
of cities, you would uncover
my grandmothers.

The scent of garlic
and the image
of a farm
in rural Ohio.
These are the forms
my grandmothers take.

The World War II nurse
and the mother of my mother
walk gently through my blood.

Dissect my cornea,
beneath the glaucoma
and macular degeneration
are my grandfathers.

The General Motors plant
and Ford assembly line
are my iris. The fishing boat
and art museum are
small pieces of metal,
microscopic cuts,
in my pupil.

Let's say none
of this makes sense.
Except for the emotion
of absence,
by which there is too much.

Rendering of my Stomach

My stomach is a pink balloon
weighed down
by Petoskey stones
and a thin layer of Lake Michigan sand.

My gut,
    where I store the guilt of unfinished books
    the phone call never returned
is soft, curved like a pear.

Always in motion
    words that spin
    fear, obsession
into a tidal wave.

Trout rise for air
and fossils flip
until smooth.

Catfish listen to the life
trapped inside the stone
as it sinks to the bottom,
then bounces.

A bowling ball,
gelatin mold,
and stray dog
flip, turn inside out.

A continuous tilt-a-whirl.

The stone coral,
a green and gray hexagon heart
that bursts
every time I forget
to breathe.

The sunset in Traverse City,
    the lake water
push up until my lungs are full
    and the sun,
the sun can be seen

in my throat.

Suspension of Memory

My brain
a gelatin mold
of matter
suspended in air.

Green olives, books of poems,
bottles of cheap wine,
    and the need to belong
hang around like kids
who wait for the morning bell
    to ring.

No focus or direction,
simply frozen.

The frontal lobe,
a creamy pink
Knox block
of attention,
holds a Christmas tree,
a blue 69 Corvette, and the family
turtle.

Emotion is invisible
but the scraps of a bungalow home,
    splintered by Michigan sand and Pittsburgh bars
    are preserved in squares of hardened gel
kept still at the front
of my brain stem

where my breath
and heart are filtered.

Each slice of clouds from the temporal lobe
    a memory
that breaks me.

Dim Sum in New York City

Egg custard buns,
pushed left to right on steel
Dim Sum carts,
like yellow centered wombs.

The soft dough jiggles,
slides against the raw crust,
until it almost breaks,
as the cart turns corners
around this dining room.

In front of me,
a small plate with a pale white orb,
soft and sticky.

It moves like a blob of fat when prodded.

Inside,
sugared egg,
cold custard,
a gel that sways as one.

Prism rays from the glass chandelier
bounce off the walls and hit
the ground.

I cut the bun
until the center oozes
out past the plate
and onto the tablecloth.

You say: *Some days, I have more hope than others.*

Cross Section of a Heart

My heart is a red velvet couch
    encased in sugar,
wrapped in red, gold, and green
lights.

Candy apple coated,
to keep the strings
and ache together.

No control of contents
    blood moves
haphazardly through valves.

Concentrated in one organ,
the fear of misdirection and disease.

Things you cannot wash away.

When I was thirteen
I touched the outside layer
of a sheep's heart with my index finger.

The fibrous organ,
gray from memory,
    the color of guilt.

The right atrium
where blood once passed
looked cold and empty.

No color present. Just cardiac cells
in need of heat or purpose.

Enlarged, sporadic beats,
anxious thumps,
are electrified in my chest.

I think only
of my heart
in color, as it pumps loud enough
for myself
to hear.

Stock of Livelihood

An organ of repression,
my filtration system,
seat of emotion,
regenerates,
but grips the past.

Heavy,
weighed down by all
that I do not acknowledge.

The unwanted
stranger's touch on my breast,
the missteps and lies
told to lovers.

All that I cannot speak,
all that I keep.

My liver recycles refrains and excuses
that point the gullible finger
at myself, and never
towards the one at fault.

Rotten, pinned down by green toxins,
words, and memory.

Panic in my liver,
there since childhood,
began with the touch on my knee,
in the church pew,
by a boy much older than me.
I learned that Sunday,
there is no peace in religion.

The red carpet, wood pews,
the ivory stand that held
baptismal water,
the candlelight that made my hands shake.

The Night Before Thanksgiving in a Trader Joe's Parking Lot

She stands in the dark parking lot,
cars honk back and forth as a teen
sings opera in the backseat of his mom's van,
windows rolled down,

this warm Asheville night.

Her camera is pointed up,
towards the heavy, navy-blue sky,
and the huge moon,
is full above us.

People rush past her,
heads down, looking ahead.

They missed it all.

American Thanksgiving

I cut the vegetables
and listen to NPR.

My husband,
studies at the table,
headphones on.

The news of bombs,
murders,
from all over the world
come into our small
North Carolina
kitchen.

I cry, as I cut the apple,
for the father who,
while on a walk with his daughter in Lebanon,
tackled the suicide bomber, saving hundreds of lives,
except his own.

There are too many losses,
a refrain that hangs in the windows.

In the oven,
I place the Thanksgiving stuffing
that we will soon bring to our friend's home
where we will drink, laugh, and return

forgetful.

The Burning of Trees, October 2017

Before the election,
before the people screamed,
trees burned.

They burned as if they already knew.

Outside our kitchen window,
the mountains cloaked
in a white haze.

A veil of ash,
dead branches,
and smoke of what used to stand tall,
is now black.

Curled fronds fall and ignite.

Scientists say that when a tree is sick
others will divert water and nutrients to the ill.

Water is scarce, the ground an incinerator.

Unearthed roots break, lose direction.
Natural highways, hundreds of years old,
cut off from one another.

The fire in the mountains turn the morning sky a pale red.
Children cannot go outside for recess and the elderly
must stay home.

This is the routine for weeks.

In months, our small backyard,
will once again be encased in trees,
though this time by fewer and thinner.

Blooms of branches
will sprout from our forearms

but the deer,

weary of humans and their absent nature,
will only show their eyes
once we become

aware.

We are the Pine Trees
for Mollie

They leave their division boards
and botany charts
to gather at the window.

The buzzing of a saw,
a new energy
felt in the classroom.

A tall pine tree
that sat below the road
for dozens of years
is being removed.

The tiny needles clog the drains
and flood the principal's office
every time it rains.

Like skin that comes in to heat
 out of December cold
their faces turn red
and their hearts thump.

The young ones stand in front,
as the older ones
come and go.

Mollie stays by the window.
Tears, dot her face,
as she turns to say:

This isn't fair.

Ask Me

Ask me about lines,
    on paper or sand,
and I will show you corners,
intersections and frost
from the night before.

Ask me and I will define borders,
    areas of transition,
where the broken sidewalks of Pittsburgh
become the Blue Ridge Mountains of Black Mountain

and choice
becomes regret.

Follow me to the lake.
I'll point out the erosion of dunes
and any other deficit made by wind.

Ask me and I will wait with you.

We will search for objects moved by invisible force:
leaves, stones, old loves.

All matter ends up somewhere,
we learn,
    through a cumulative force
        of our own

      or nature's accord.

Driving to East Lansing for my Brother's Intervention

We stop at a diner,
order greasy pancakes
and drink coffee from a brown carafe.

Mom shakes her head,
cries through a mumbled:
I don't know what to do. He's so angry, all the time.

Dad keeps to himself. Takes a picture of my sister and me.

A way to remember the day, he said.

Diorama

A room of dried leaves,
soup bowls in a bathroom sink,
    and you
shirtless on my couch
as you watch Netflix
for five days
straight.

Stars that have given up
hang before your eyes.

A morning moon
that doesn't know
where it belongs
sits next to you.

It is winter in my studio apartment.

We stay no more than twenty feet
from each other.

I circle you,
carry empty plates to the kitchen,
    pancakes in the morning,
    lasagna in the evening,
then return
to watch you,
watch me.

We are busy
sweeping vines
from polka dot trees
out the window.

The extra whales
we place on the mantel.

We are the corners
where nothing clean
ever collects.

Suttons Bay, MI

Bring me to the cherries
of Northern Michigan
and the stranger's orchard
where we sat in lawn chairs
and drank beer
as the sun set.

Place in my hand
the firm bulb of fruit
where entire stories,
timelines of life,
are preserved.

Let me bite down on the myth
that surrounds the pit
and let it drip
down my fingers.

There is so much
we do not believe in

least of all
home

but the cherries,

the cherries are where
I wish to be.

Are You a Member of the Co-Op?

He stood outside the co-op
wire rimmed glasses, jeans, and burnt orange shirt
a name tag that read, Glen.

The Co-Op is doing away with the volunteer program, he said.

I normally don't stop for petitions
but he was warm, soft-spoken, and confident.

As he held the clipboard
and listed the benefits of a volunteer program
       all of which I agreed with
I imagined myself in Vermont with Glen
in a cabin
sitting next to a fireplace
as he drank his bourbon and I
drank a beer.

He would look up from his newspaper,
take off his glasses,
put his hand on my leg,
and say: *It's almost 11, should we go to bed?*

Before I could answer,
he would grab my hand
finish my beer
and kiss my neck.

On the street in Pittsburgh,
I stare at his face
the lines around his mouth
his clear skin.

He must not be a smoker.
Who knows if he even drinks?

As he finished talking
thoughts of Vermont were still
in the corners of my eyes as I said:

Yes. I would love to sign your petition.

And all he could say was:
Thank you.

Berlin is a City of Borders

Berlin is a city of twin beds
pushed together at night
and a friend
I no longer hear from.

It is a city of grocery stores
so efficient and bare boned
that even a lost tourist
can find sugar free jelly
in aisle 10, on the second floor.

Berlin is a dead-end street
where we sleep
book ended by a cemetery
and Italian market.

It is the city where you
laid beside me,
talked me to sleep,
but kept your distance.

Berlin is twenty German words
shared between two American friends
who studied literature and the need
to hold on.

It is a city of self-cleaning
public restrooms and cheap
falafel pitas, outside
the S-Bahn station.

Berlin is East
and West
trying to push closer together
so that borders disappear.

We do the same
but fail.

Stefanie Wielkopolan is a native Michigander who now calls Pittsburgh, PA home. Up until the age of eight, she spent every Saturday watching cartoons at a bowling alley bar. She credits this experience for her love of a good dive bar, people watching, and writing poetry. She holds a Master's of Liberal Studies from the University of Michigan-Dearborn and a Master's of Fine Arts in Poetry from Chatham University. Her first collection of poetry, *Border Theory*, was published by Black Coffee Press in 2011.

www.ingramcontent.com/pod-product-compliance
Lightning Source LLC
Chambersburg PA
CBHW022124090426
42743CB00008B/994